BOOK 2 - B♭ Clarinet

STANDARD OF EXCELLENCE

ENHANCED COMPREHENSIVE BAND METHOD

By Bruce Pearson

Dear Student:

Congratulations! You have successfully attained the first level in achieving a standard of excellence in music-making. By now, you have discovered that careful study and regular practice have brought you the joy and satisfaction of making beautiful music.

You are now ready to move to the next level in your music-making. I want to welcome you to STANDARD OF EXCELLENCE ENHANCED, Book 2. I also want to wish you continued success and enjoyment.

Best wishes,

Bruce Pearson

Practice and Assessment - the key to EXCELLENCE!

▶ Make practicing part of your daily schedule. If you plan it as you do any other activity, you will find plenty of time for it.
▶ Try to practice in the same place every day. Choose a place where you can concentrate on making music. Start with a regular and familiar warm-up routine, including long tones and simple technical exercises. Like an athlete, you need to warm-up your mind and muscles before you begin performing.
▶ Always tune before you play. Use the tuning tracks found on the Accompaniment Recordings, or use the *iPAS* Tuner.
▶ Set goals for every practice session. Keep track of your practice time and progress on the front cover Practice Journal.
▶ Practice the difficult spots in your lesson assignment and band music over and over at a slower tempo, until you can play them perfectly, then gradually increase the tempo. Use the *iPAS* Metronome to track your progress and ensure you are playing with a steady pulse.
▶ Spend time practicing alone and with the Accompaniment Recordings.
▶ Assess your progress and achievements by using *iPAS*. Listen to the recordings you create to hear the spots in the music which might need improvement.
▶ At the end of each practice session, play something fun!

ISBN 0-8497-0771-4

KJOS NEIL A. KJOS MUSIC COMPANY, PUBLISHER   PW22CL

REVIEW

C MAJOR KEY SIGNATURE

1 WARM-UP - Band Arrangement
Andante

2 C MAJOR SCALE SKILL (Concert B♭ Major)
Moderato

▶ Lines with a medal are *Achievement Lines.* The chart on page 47 can be used to record your progress.

3 BOTANY BAY Page 40 Australian Folk Song
Moderato

▶ When you see a page number followed by an arrow, *Excellerate* to the page indicated for additional studies.

4 DRIVE TIME
Andante

5 SHEPHERD'S HEY English Folk Song
Moderato *Fine*

D.C. al Fine

REVIEW

F MAJOR KEY SIGNATURE

6 F MAJOR SCALE SKILL (Concert E♭ Major)

Moderato — Arpeggio — Chords div.

mf

▶ Are you playing with a good embouchure and hand position?

7 MOLLY MALONE

Irish Folk Song

Andante

mp — *f* — *mp* — *rit.* — *mp*

1. 2.

8 NO LOOKING BACK

Page 40

Moderato

mf

9 TURKISH MARCH

Wolfgang Amadeus Mozart (1756-1791)

Allegro

mf

1. 2.

10 HYMN OF THANKSGIVING - Band Arrangement

Johann Crüger (1598-1662)
arr. Bruce Pearson (b. 1942)

Andante div.

mf — *p* — *mf*

p

f — *mf rit.*

REVIEW

G MAJOR KEY SIGNATURE

11 WARM-UP - Band Arrangement

Andante

12 G MAJOR SCALE SKILL (Concert F Major)

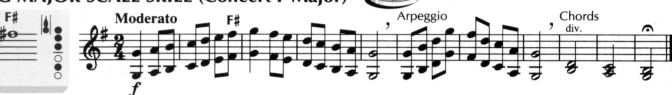

13 KNUCKLEBUSTER

14 GIVE ME THAT OLD TIME RELIGION

Page 40 ▐▐▐▐▶

American Spiritual

15 _____   Composer _____

your name

▶ Compose an ending for this melody. Title and play your composition.

16 FOR CLARINETS ONLY

Page 40 ▐▐▐▐▶

▶ *Use the alternate F♯ fingering when moving from F♮ to F♯ or F♯ to F♮.

PW22CL

| SYNCOPATION |  | A rhythmic effect which places emphasis on a weak or unaccented part of the measure. |
| INTERVAL | | The distance between any two notes. |

17 SYNCOPATION SENSATION

18 THE RIDDLE SONG

American Folk Song

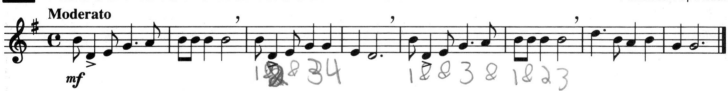

▶ Write in the counting and clap the rhythm before you play.

19 NOBODY KNOWS THE TROUBLE I'VE SEEN

American Spiritual

20 INTERVAL INQUIRY

▶ Sing this exercise using the numbers before you play.

21 GO FOR EXCELLENCE!

American Folk Song

PW22CL

A MINOR KEY SIGNATURE	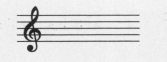	**A minor** has the same key signature as **C major**.
TEMPO		*Accelerando (accel.)* - Gradually increase the tempo.

22 WARM-UP - Band Arrangement

Andante

23 A NATURAL MINOR SCALE SKILL (Concert G Natural Minor)

24 A HARMONIC MINOR SCALE SKILL (Concert G Harmonic Minor)

25 MINKA, MINKA   Page 40 ▶

Ukrainian Folk Song

2nd time - *accel.*   Hey!

26 LAREDO - Duet

Mexican Folk Song

▶ Name the interval between the top and bottom notes of the last measure. _____

27 TURNING YOU LOOSE

28 FOR CLARINETS ONLY

Andante

DAL SEGNO AL FINE (D.S. AL FINE)

Go back to the sign (𝄋) and play until the *Fine.*

JOYEUX NOËL
Band Arrangement

French Carol
arr. Chuck Elledge (b. 1961)

29 GO FOR EXCELLENCE!

EIGHTH REST

𝄽

𝄽 = ½ count in **2/4**, **3/4**, and **4/4** time.

An eighth rest is as long as an eighth note.

30 EIGHTH REST ON THE BEAT
Moderato

mf

▶ Write in the counting and clap the rhythm before you play.

31 EIGHTH REST OFF THE BEAT
Moderato

f

32 ACADEMIC FESTIVAL MARCH - Trio   Johannes Brahms (1833-1897)
Moderato

A. *f*

B. *f*

C. *f*

33 BREEZIN'
Allegro

p

34 YANKEE DOODLE - Duet   American Folk Song
Moderato

A. *mf*

B. *mf*

35 FOR CLARINETS ONLY

Andante
G#

G#

f

PW22CL

B♭ MAJOR KEY SIGNATURE	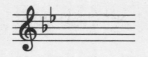	This key signature means play all B's as B flats and all E's as E flats.
TEXTURES		**Monophony** - a single unaccompanied melody. **Polyphony** - two or more melodies played at the same time.

36 B♭ MAJOR SCALE SKILL (Concert A♭ Major)

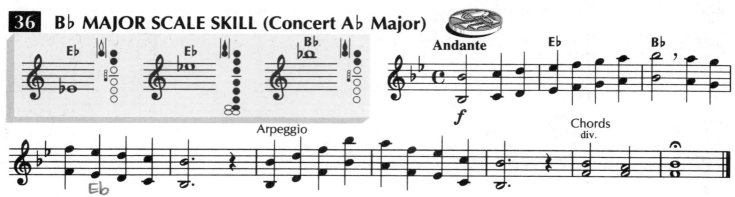

▶ Try playing both octaves.

37 GREASED LIGHTNING Page 40 ▶

38 PARTNER SONGS - Duet

▶ For an example of monophony, play line A or line B alone. For an example of polyphony, play line A while someone else plays line B.

39 GO FOR EXCELLENCE! Stephen Foster (1826-1864)

PW22CL

ENHARMONICS	ARTICULATION	TEMPO
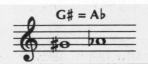 G# = Ab		**Allegretto -** light and lively; slightly slower than **Allegro.**
Notes that sound the same but are written differently.	*Staccato* (dot placed above or below note) - Play short and detached.	

40 **WARM-UP - Band Arrangement**

41 **CHROMATIC CAPERS**

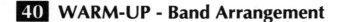

▶ *Use the alternate F# fingering.

42 **SHENANDOAH**

American Folk Song

43 **THEME FROM SYMPHONY NO. 94**

Franz Joseph Haydn (1732-1809)

44 **PARADE OF THE TIN SOLDIERS**

Léon Jessel (1871-1942)

45 **FOR CLARINETS ONLY**

Page 40 ▶▶▶▶

▶ *Use the alternate C fingering.

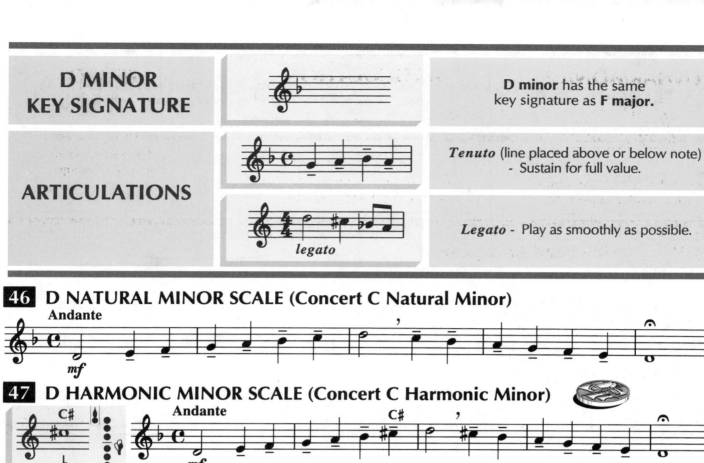

D MINOR KEY SIGNATURE		**D minor** has the same key signature as **F major**.
ARTICULATIONS		*Tenuto* (line placed above or below note) - Sustain for full value.
	legato	*Legato* - Play as smoothly as possible.

46 **D NATURAL MINOR SCALE (Concert C Natural Minor)**
Andante

47 **D HARMONIC MINOR SCALE (Concert C Harmonic Minor)**
Andante

48 **MARCHE SLAV**
Peter Ilyich Tchaikovsky (1840-1893)
Andante

49 **GREENSLEEVES**
English Song
Moderato

▶ Name the key in "Greensleeves." _____

50 **JUBILATE**
Wolfgang Amadeus Mozart (1756-1791)
Allegretto

51 **GO FOR EXCELLENCE!**
Allegretto

▶ *Use the alternate C fingering.

TEXTURE

Melody and Accompaniment - main melody is accompanied by chords or less important melodies called **countermelodies.**

52 WARM-UP

Andante

mf legato

53 HABAÑERA

Georges Bizet (1838-1875)

Andante

mf

54 SMOOTH AS SILK

Allegretto

f

55 HEY HO - Round (Canon)

Medieval Song

Allegro

f

56 THE BRITISH GRENADIERS - Duet Page 40

English Folk Song

Allegro

A. Melody

f

B. Countermelody

f

57 FOR CLARINETS ONLY

Eb alternate

Bb alternate

A Moderato

mf

B

▶ *Use the alternate fingerings for Eb and Bb.

TIME SIGNATURE

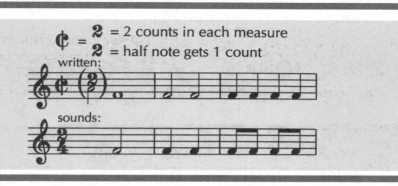

This time signature is called **cut time** or *alla breve*.

58 CUT AND PASTE

Moderato

▶ Write in the counting and clap the rhythm before you play.

59 OATS, PEAS, BEANS

American Folk Song

Moderato

A.

mf

B.

mf

60 THE VICTORS

Fight Song

Allegro

f

61 OVER EASY Page 41 ▮▮▮▶

Andante

f

62 GO FOR EXCELLENCE!

John Philip Sousa (1854-1932)

Allegretto

"High School Cadets March"

mp

mf

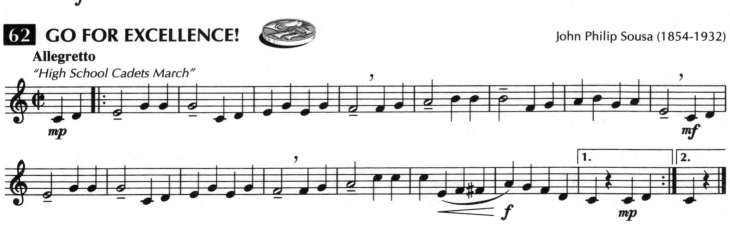

f

mp

ENHARMONICS

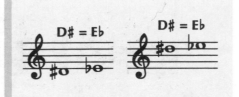

CHORD

fifth
third
root

Two or more pitches sounded at the same time.

63 WARM-UP - Band Arrangement

64 DANISH ROLL   Page 41   Danish Folk Song

65 RUSSIAN SAILORS' DANCE   Reinhold Glière (1875-1956)

66 CHORD CAPERS

▶ Listen for the different types of chords played by the full band. The clarinets are playing two notes of each chord.

67 FOR CLARINETS ONLY

ENHARMONICS

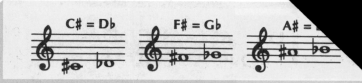

C# = Db   F# = Gb   A# =

---

68 CHROMATIC SCALE SKILL

Andante

A#

Gb   Db

▶ *Use the alternate F#/Gb fingering.

---

69 SAILING THE HIGH SEAS

Moderato

mp   mf   f

mf

---

70 CHROMATIC MARCH

Allegro

f

p - 1st time
f - 2nd time

1.

2.

---

71 MANHATTAN BEACH MARCH

John Philip Sousa (1854-1932)

Allegro

mf

---

72 GO FOR EXCELLENCE!

Moderato

mf

▶ Play using each of the following articulations: A.   B.   C.   D.

APO AL CODA
C. AL CODA)

Go back to the beginning and play until the coda sign (⊕). When you reach the coda sign, skip to the *Coda* (⊕).

ROCK ISLAND EXPRESS
Band Arrangement

Chuck Elledge (b. 1961)

TIME SIGNATURE	$\frac{3}{8}$	**3** = 3 counts in each measure **8** = eighth note gets 1 count

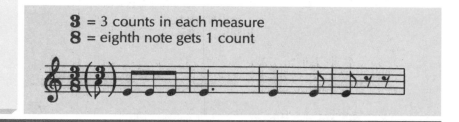

73 _____   Composer _____

your name

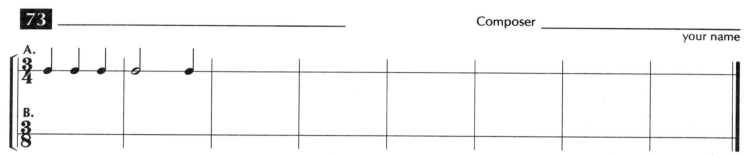

▶ Compose an ending for the $\frac{3}{4}$ rhythm composition on line **A**. Title your composition, then count and clap it.

▶ On line **B**, rewrite your composition in $\frac{3}{8}$. Count and clap it.

74 TRIPLE PLAY

▶ Write in the counting and clap the rhythm before you play.

75 WE THREE KINGS

John H. Hopkins, Jr. (1820-1891)

▶ Name the key in "We Three Kings." _____

76 GO FOR EXCELLENCE!

 **D MAJOR KEY SIGNATURE**

This key signature means play all F's as F sharps and all C's as C sharps.

TIME SIGNATURE $\frac{6}{8}$

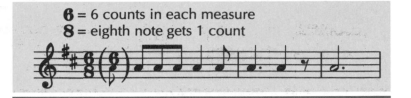

6 = 6 counts in each measure
8 = eighth note gets 1 count

---

77 D MAJOR SCALE SKILL (Concert C Major)

Arpeggio   Chords div.

▶ *Refer to the third C♯ fingering (R) on the fingering chart found on the inside back cover of this book.

78 OVER THE RIVER Page 41 ▶ Traditional

▶ Draw in a breath mark at the end of each phrase.

79 OODLES OF NOODLES

▶ Use the right hand fingering for all C♯'s in the staff.

80 UPS AND DOWNS

▶ Write in the counting and draw in the bar lines before you play.

81 FOR CLARINETS ONLY   Page 41 ▶

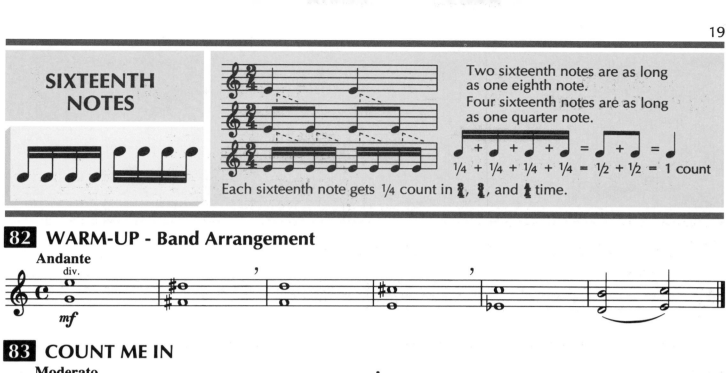

SIXTEENTH NOTES

Two sixteenth notes are as long as one eighth note.
Four sixteenth notes are as long as one quarter note.

$\frac{1}{4} + \frac{1}{4} + \frac{1}{4} + \frac{1}{4} = \frac{1}{2} + \frac{1}{2} = 1$ count

Each sixteenth note gets ¼ count in 𝄴, 𝄵, and 𝄵 time.

82 WARM-UP - Band Arrangement

Andante

83 COUNT ME IN

Moderato

▶ Write in the counting and clap the rhythm before you play.

84 KEMO KIMO

American Folk Song

Allegretto

85 FRENCH MARCHING SONG

French Folk Song

Allegro

▶ Name the interval between the first and second notes. _____

86 FENG YANG SONG   Page 41 ▐▐▐▶

Chinese Folk Song

Moderato

87 GO FOR EXCELLENCE!

Patrick Gilmore (1829-1892)

Allegro

"When Johnny Comes Marching Home"

88 LOOBY LOO

Anonymous

Allegro

mf

Fine

D.C. al Fine

▶ Name the key in "Looby Loo." _____

89 THE THUNDERER

John Philip Sousa (1854-1932)

Allegretto

f

90 LISTEN TO THE MOCKINGBIRD

Alice Hawthorne (1827-1902)

Moderato

f   *mp*   *f*

91 GIVE MY REGARDS TO BROADWAY

George M. Cohan (1878-1942)

Allegro

to Coda

f

D.C. al Coda

Coda

92 FOR CLARINETS ONLY

Page 41 ▶

Andante

EIGHTH/SIXTEENTH NOTE COMBINATIONS

93 **CHESTER - Band Arrangement**

William Billings (1746-1800)
arr. Bruce Pearson (b. 1942)

94 **STEADY AS YOU GO - Duet**

95 **TIRRA LIRRA LOO**

Canadian Folk Song

▶ Write in the counting and clap the rhythm before you play.

96 **GO FOR EXCELLENCE!**

American Folk Song

Moderato
"Big Rock Candy Mountain"

22

The written piano accompaniment
for TURKISH MARCH is included on
track 1 of CD 2 for easy access in a
performance situation.

TURKISH MARCH
from "The Ruins of Athens"
Solo with Piano Accompaniment

Ludwig van Beethoven (1770-1827)
arr. Bruce Pearson (b. 1942)

97 BLAZIN'

▶ Name the interval between the first and second notes. _____

98 AMERICAN PATROL   Frank W. Meacham (1856-1909)

99 KERRY DANCE   Irish Folk Song

100 GAVOTTE   James Hook (1746-1827)

101 FOR CLARINETS ONLY   Page 41

▶ *Use the alternate fingerings for E♭ and high B♭.

SINGLE SIXTEENTH NOTE

A single sixteenth note is half as long as an eighth note.

♬ = ¼ count in ₂, ₃, and ₄ time.

DOTTED EIGHTH NOTE

A dot after a note adds half the value of the note.

♪ + · = ♪ + ♪ = ♪♪

DOTTED EIGHTH/ SIXTEENTH NOTE COMBINATION

102 DOTS OF FUN

103 LITTLE BROWN JUG - Duet

Joseph Eastburn Winner (1837-1918)

▶ Write in the counting and clap the rhythm before you play.

104 OUR BOYS WILL SHINE TONIGHT

College Song

▶ Draw in a breath mark at the end of each phrase.

105 _____   Composer _____
your name

▶ Compose an ending for this melody. Be sure to use the ♪· ♬ rhythm. Title and play your composition.

106 GO FOR EXCELLENCE!

Georges Bizet (1838-1875)

"Farandole from L'Arlesienne Suite"

PW22CL

26

107 CUCKOO SONG

Austrian Folk Song

108 MARCH MILITAIRE

Page 41 ▐▐▐➤

Franz Schubert (1797-1828)

to Coda ⊕

D.C. al Coda ⊕ *Coda*

109 ST. ANTHONY CHORALE

Franz Joseph Haydn (1732-1809)

Fine

D.C. al Fine

▶ *Use the alternate C fingering.

110 _____

Composer _____
your name

▶ Arrange these melodic pieces in any order to build a tune you like. You may use pieces more than once. Title and play your composition.

111 FOR CLARINETS ONLY

PW22CL

EIGHTH NOTE TRIPLET

$$\frac{1}{3} + \frac{1}{3} + \frac{1}{3} = \frac{2}{3} + \frac{1}{3} = 1 \text{ count in } \frac{2}{4}, \frac{3}{4}, \text{ and } \frac{4}{4} \text{ time.}$$

TEMPO

Maestoso - majestically

112 TRIPLE TREAT

113 STARS OF THE HEAVENS - Duet

Mexican Folk Song

114 LIGHT CAVALRY OVERTURE

Franz von Suppé (1819-1895)

115 GO FOR EXCELLENCE!

Charles Gounod (1818-1893)

"Soldiers' Chorus from Faust"

116 HERE WE COME A-WASSAILING

English Folk Song

117 THEME FROM "ZAMPA"

Ferdinand Herold (1791-1833)

118 GO FOR EXCELLENCE!

Peter Ilyich Tchaikovsky (1840-1893)

"March from the Nutcracker"

CABO RICO
Band Arrangement

Chuck Elledge (b. 1961)

RUDIMENTAL REGIMENT

Band Arrangement

Bruce Pearson (b. 1942)
and Chuck Elledge (b. 1961)

SUMMER'S RAIN
Band Arrangement

Chuck Elledge (b. 1961)

FRENCH MARKET BUZZARDS MARCH
Band Arrangement

Liberato Gallo
arr. Wendy Barden (b. 1955)

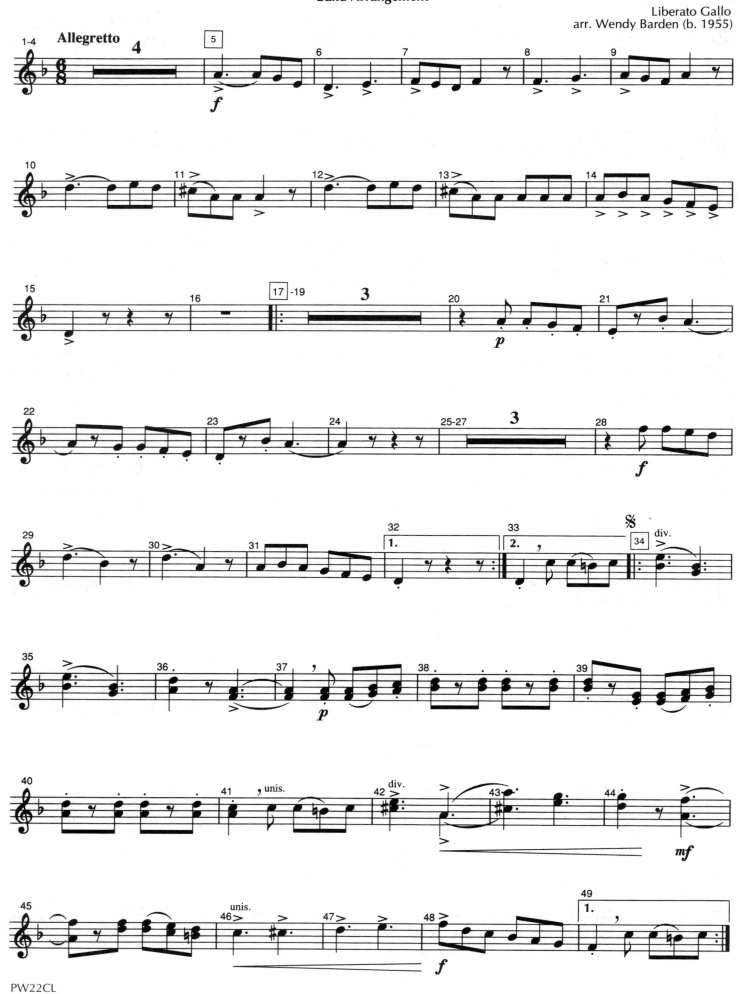

ROMANZA
Ensemble

Ludwig van Beethoven, Op. 40 (1770-1827)
arr. Janice Strobl Kersey (b. 1959)

Part A

HORNPIPE from "Water Music"
Ensemble

George Frideric Handel (1685-1759)
arr. Janice Strobl Kersey (b. 1959)

Part A

The written piano accompaniment for FINALE is included on track 6 of CD 2. You will hear a 2-measure click before you play to help you get started.

FINALE
from String Quartet Op. 74, No. 2
Solo with Piano Accompaniment

Franz Joseph Haydn (1732-1809)
arr. Bruce Pearson (b. 1942)

EXCELLERATORS-FOR CLARINETS ONLY

▶ Keep your right hand down for all notes above the RHD⌐⌐.

▶ *Use the alternate F♯ fingering.

▶ *Use the alternate B♮ fingering.

▶ *Use the alternate C fingering.

EXCELLERATORS-FOR CLARINETS ONLY

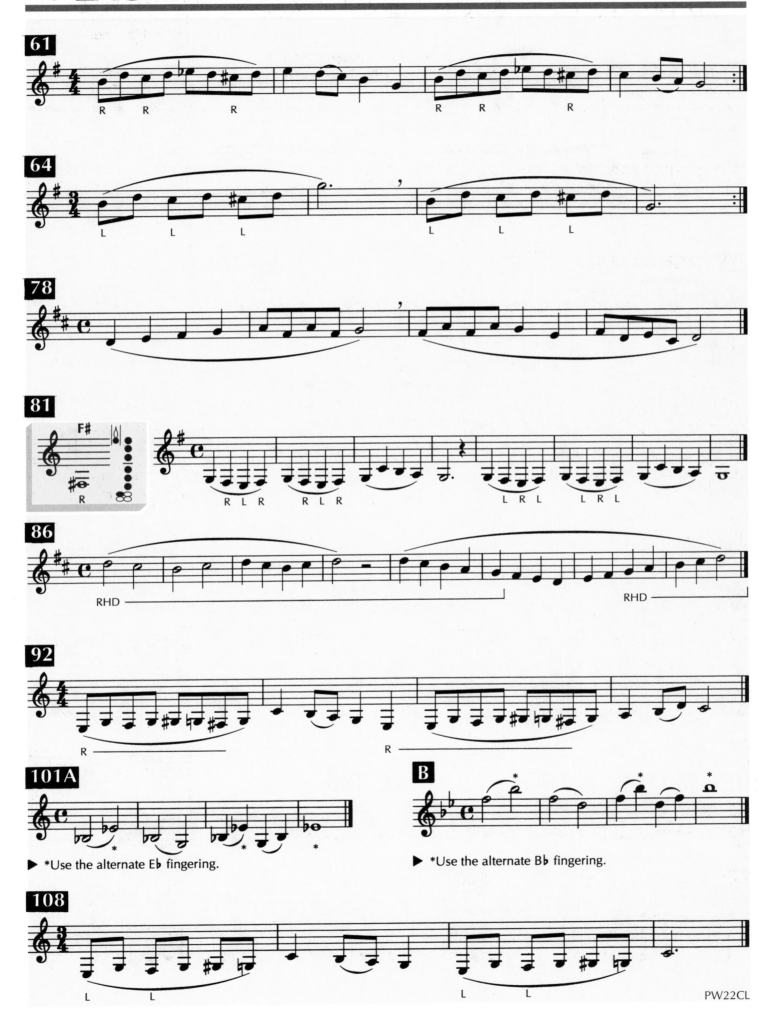

▶ *Use the alternate E♭ fingering.

▶ *Use the alternate B♭ fingering.

SCALE STUDIES

C MAJOR SCALE (Concert B♭ Major)

Arpeggio

Thirds

A HARMONIC MINOR SCALE (Concert G Harmonic Minor)

Arpeggio

Thirds

F MAJOR SCALE (Concert E♭ Major)

Arpeggio

Thirds

D HARMONIC MINOR SCALE (Concert C Harmonic Minor)

Arpeggio

Thirds

SCALE STUDIES

G MAJOR SCALE (Concert F Major)

Bb MAJOR SCALE (Concert Ab Major)

D MAJOR SCALE (Concert C Major)

CHROMATIC SCALE

RHYTHM STUDIES

RHYTHM STUDIES

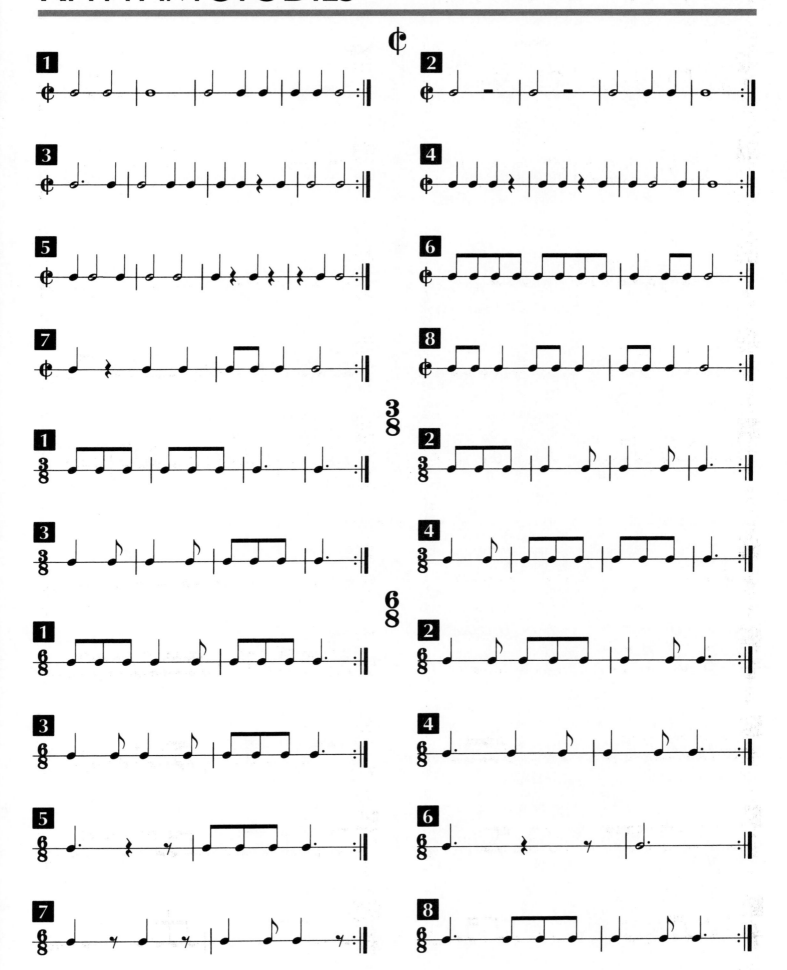

GLOSSARY/INDEX

Accelerando *(accel.)* (p.6) . . . . gradually increase the tempo

Alla Breve (p.13) . . . . same as cut time

Allegretto (p.10) . . . . light and lively; slightly slower than **Allegro**

Barden, Wendy (pp.34-35) . . . . American music educator and arranger *(b. 1955)*

Beethoven, Ludwig van (pp.22-23, 36-37). German composer *(1770-1827)*

Billings, William (p.21) . . . . American composer *(1746-1800)*

Bizet, Georges (pp.12, 25) . . . . French composer *(1838-1875)*

Brahms, Johannes (p.8) . . . . German composer *(1833-1897)*

Chord (pp.2-4, 9, 14, 18) . . . . two or more pitches sounded at the same time

Chromatic Scale (pp.15, 43) . . . . . . scale of half steps

Cohan, George M. (p.20) . . . . American composer *(1878-1942)*

Countermelody (p.12) . . . . a less important melody that can be played along with the main melody

Crüger, Johann (p.3) . . . . German composer *(1598-1662)*

Cut Time *(alla breve)* (p.13) ¢ or ⅔ . . . a time signature indicating two counts in each measure, the half note gets one count

Da Capo al Coda (p.16) *D.C. al Coda* . . go back to the beginning and play until the coda sign (⊕). When you reach the coda sign, skip to the *Coda* (⊕)

Dal Segno al Fine (p.7) *D.S. al Fine* . . go back to the 𝄋 sign and play until the *Fine*

Elledge, Chuck (pp.7, 16, 29-33) . . . American composer/arranger *(b.1961)*

Enharmonics (pp.10, 14-15) . . . . notes that sound the same but are written differently

Foster, Stephen (p.9) . . . . American composer *(1826-1864)*

Gallo, Liberato (pp.34-35) . . . . Italian composer

Gilmore, Patrick (p.19) . . . . American composer *(1829-1892)*

Glière, Reinhold (p.14) . . . . Russian composer *(1875-1956)*

Gounod, Charles (p.27) . . . . French composer *(1818-1893)*

Handel, George Frideric (p.37) . . . . . German composer *(1685-1759)*

Hawthorne, Alice (p.20) . . . . American composer *(1827-1902)*

Haydn, Franz Joseph (pp.10, 26, 38-39) . Austrian composer *(1732-1809)*

Herold, Ferdinand (p.28) . . . . French composer *(1791-1833)*

Hook, James (p.24) . . . . English composer *(1746-1827)*

Hopkins, John H., Jr. (p.17) . . . . American composer *(1820-1891)*

Interval (p.5) . . . . distance between two notes

Jessel, Léon (p.10) . . . . German composer *(1871-1942)*

Kersey, Janice Strobl (pp.36-37) . . . . . American music editor and arranger *(b.1959)*

Legato (p.11) . . . . play as smoothly as possible

Maestoso (p.27) . . . . majestically

Meacham, Frank W. (p.24) . . . . American composer *(1856-1909)*

Melody (p.12) . . . . an organized succession of tones

Monophony (p.9) . . . . a single unaccompanied melody

Mozart, Wolfgang Amadeus (pp.3,11) . . Austrian composer *(1756-1791)*

Pearson, Bruce . . . . American music educator/composer/ arranger *(b.1942)*

Polyphony (p.9) . . . . two or more melodies played at the same time

Schubert, Franz (p.26) . . . . Austrian composer *(1797-1828)*

Sousa, John Philip (pp.13, 15, 20) . . . . . American composer *(1854-1932)*

Staccato (p.10) ♩ . . . . a dot placed above or below note meaning to play short and detached

Suppé, Franz von (p.27) . . . . Belgian composer *(1819-1895)*

Syncopation (p.5) ♪♩♪ . . . . a rhythmic effect which places emphasis on a weak or unaccented part of the measure

Tchaikovsky, Peter Ilyich (pp.11, 28) . . . . Russian composer *(1840-1893)*

Tenuto (p.11) ♩ . . . . a line placed above or below note meaning to sustain for full value

Texture (p.12) . . . . the character of a composition as determined by the relationship of its melodies, countermelodies, and/or chords

Unison (p.6) . . . . everyone plays the same notes

Winner, Joseph Eastburn (p.25) . . . . . . American composer *(1837-1918)*

STANDARD OF

EXERCISE 2
- [ ] notes/rhythm
- [ ] posture
- [ ] embouchure
- [ ] breathing

EXERCISE 5
- [ ] notes/rhythm
- [ ] dynamics
- [ ] articulations
- [ ] *D. C. al Fine*

EXERCISE 6
- [ ] notes/rhythm
- [ ] hand position
- [ ] breathing
- [ ] tone

EXERCISE 7
- [ ] notes/rhythm
- [ ] *ritardando*
- [ ] dynamics
- [ ] 1st/2nd endings

EXERCISE 12
- [ ] notes/rhythm
- [ ] posture
- [ ] hand position
- [ ] breathing

EXERCISE 16
- [ ] notes/rhythm
- [ ] embouchure
- [ ] hand position
- [ ] tone

EXERCISE 21
- [ ] notes/rhythm
- [ ] hand position
- [ ] dynamics
- [ ] tempo

EXERCISE 24
- [ ] notes/rhythm
- [ ] embouchure
- [ ] 𝄐
- [ ] tone

EXERCISE 28
- [ ] notes/rhythm
- [ ] posture
- [ ] hand position
- [ ] tone

EXERCISE 29
- [ ] notes/rhythm
- [ ] embouchure
- [ ] breathing
- [ ] *D. C. al Fine*

EXERCISE 33
- [ ] notes/rhythm
- [ ] hand position
- [ ] dynamics
- [ ] tone

EXERCISE 35
- [ ] notes/rhythm
- [ ] breathing
- [ ] tempo
- [ ] tone

EXERCISE 36
- [ ] notes/rhythm
- [ ] posture
- [ ] embouchure
- [ ] tone

EXERCISE 39
- [ ] notes/rhythm
- [ ] embouchure
- [ ] dynamics
- [ ] *accelerando*

EXERCISE 42
- [ ] notes/rhythm
- [ ] hand position
- [ ] time signatures
- [ ] 𝄐

EXERCISE 45
- [ ] notes/rhythm
- [ ] hand position
- [ ] articulation
- [ ] tone

EXERCISE 47
- [ ] notes/rhythm
- [ ] posture
- [ ] tenuto
- [ ] tone

EXERCISE 51
- [ ] notes/rhythm
- [ ] hand position
- [ ] articulation
- [ ] tempo

EXERCISE 53
- [ ] notes/rhythm
- [ ] embouchure
- [ ] accents
- [ ] tempo

EXERCISE 57
- [ ] notes/rhythm
- [ ] hand position
- [ ] embouchure
- [ ] tone

EXERCISE 62
- [ ] notes/rhythm
- [ ] dynamics
- [ ] tenuto
- [ ] tempo

EXERCISE 65
- [ ] notes/rhythm
- [ ] posture
- [ ] articulations
- [ ] *D. C. al Fine*

EXERCISE 67
- [ ] notes/rhythm
- [ ] hand position
- [ ] embouchure
- [ ] tone

EXERCISE 69
- [ ] notes/rhythm
- [ ] hand position
- [ ] embouchure
- [ ] tone

EXERCISE 72
- [ ] notes/rhythm
- [ ] posture
- [ ] articulations
- [ ] breathing

EXERCISE 76
- [ ] notes/rhythm
- [ ] tempo
- [ ] legato
- [ ] tone

EXERCISE 77
- [ ] notes/rhythm
- [ ] hand position
- [ ] tempo
- [ ] tone

EXERCISE 81
- [ ] notes/rhythm
- [ ] hand position
- [ ] embouchure
- [ ] tone

EXERCISE 87
- [ ] notes/rhythm
- [ ] dynamics
- [ ] tone
- [ ] tempo

EXERCISE 88
- [ ] notes/rhythm
- [ ] hand position
- [ ] time signatures
- [ ] tonguing

EXERCISE 91
- [ ] notes/rhythm
- [ ] *D. C. al Coda*
- [ ] tempo
- [ ] tone

EXERCISE 92
- [ ] notes/rhythm
- [ ] hand position
- [ ] posture
- [ ] tone

EXERCISE 96
- [ ] notes/rhythm
- [ ] dynamics
- [ ] accents
- [ ] tonguing

EXERCISE 100
- [ ] notes/rhythm
- [ ] dynamics
- [ ] articulations
- [ ] tempo

EXERCISE 101
- [ ] notes/rhythm
- [ ] hand position
- [ ] posture
- [ ] tone

EXERCISE 106
- [ ] notes/rhythm
- [ ] accents
- [ ] tempo
- [ ] tone

EXERCISE 111
- [ ] notes/rhythm
- [ ] tempo
- [ ] posture
- [ ] tone

EXERCISE 115
- [ ] notes/rhythm
- [ ] hand position
- [ ] tempo
- [ ] accents

EXERCISE 116
- [ ] notes/rhythm
- [ ] time signatures
- [ ] tempo
- [ ] articulations

EXERCISE 118
- [ ] notes/rhythm
- [ ] articulations
- [ ] tempo
- [ ] tone

EXCELLENCE

THE B♭ CLARINET

CLARINET CHECKLIST

☐ Sitting up straight
☐ Right and left thumbs correctly placed
☐ Clarinet in center of body with bell between knees
☐ Clarinet at correct angle
☐ Head erect
☐ Fingers gently curved
☐ Wrists straight
☐ Elbows away from body
☐ Mouthpiece proper distance in mouth
☐ Top teeth resting directly on mouthpiece
☐ Equal pressure on all sides of mouthpiece
☐ Chin flat and pointed
☐ Breathing correctly by inhaling through corners of mouth
☐ Good tone produced

CLARINET SURVIVAL KIT

☐ swab   ☐ soft, clean cloth
☐ extra reeds   ☐ reed holder
☐ cork grease   ☐ pencil
☐ method book   ☐ band music
☐ music stand

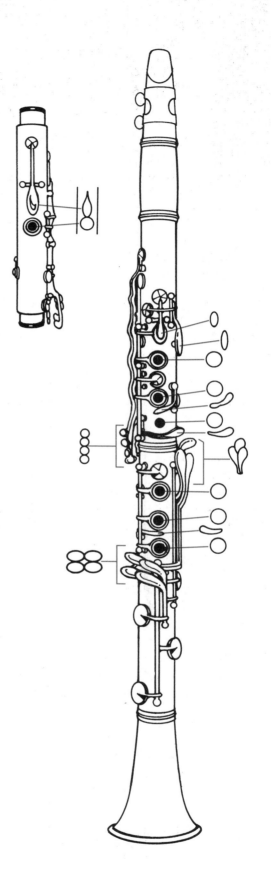